Alligator

by

Theresa Breslin

Illustrated by Shona Grant

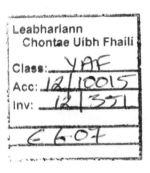
First published in 2008 in Great Britain by
Barrington Stoke Ltd
18 Walker St, Edinburgh, EH3 7LP

www.barringtonstoke.co.uk

Reprinted 2009

ISBN: 978-1-84299-522-8

Printed in Great Britain by Bell & Bain Ltd

A Note from the Author

The words jumped out at me when I picked up the newspaper – "Police called as man tries to sell alligator at a car boot sale." Right away I thought: Hey! That would be a terrific way to begin a story. I could just picture the scene – someone whispering as people went past, "Psst! Wanna buy an alligator?"

I wondered … what kind of person would try to sell an alligator at a car boot sale? So I invented a character called Crusher. I also wondered … who would buy an alligator at a car boot sale? That gave me my main character. I called him Jono.

I really like Jono. He's the same as me. He doesn't mean to get himself into a mess but things just happen to him.

Then I thought … what would Jono do with the alligator when he got it home?

You'll have to read the story to find out ….

This book is for Callum

Contents

Chapter 1

Wanna Buy an Alligator?

"*Pssst!* Wanna buy an alligator?"

"What?" I turned my head.

I saw Crusher standing by his car. The boot lid was open.

"Jono," he said. "I've got something here, just for you."

I went over.

Crusher had this long box in his car boot.

"Look, Jono," he said. "Look inside."

He lifted the lid.

The thing inside was about a metre long. It was covered up with straw so at first I couldn't see it very well.

But then it moved and I saw what it was.

An alligator.

Chapter 2

Alligators Are Great Pets

"An alligator!" I said. "No way."

I began to walk away but Crusher grabbed my arm.

"Wait up, Jono," he said. "An alligator is a great pet, so it is. And if you don't like it you can always turn it into a pair of shoes."

"If it's so great why are you selling it?" I asked him.

That's the first thing you should always ask when someone tries to sell you something. My dad told me that. Before he went and died. Always ask the seller, *"Why are you selling this?"*

"Why are you selling this alligator?"
I asked Crusher.

"I'm selling it for a friend," said Crusher.

"Where did he get it?" I asked.

"His mum brought it back from Australia
or China or somewhere."

"What?" I said. It seemed a bit odd to me,
that.

"I know, I know," said Crusher. "Other
folk's mums bring back T-shirts, but my pal's

mum brought him back this alligator. Now he don't want it, and he asked me to sell it for him."

I wasn't falling for this one. "How did his mum get it past the security checks?"

"She put it in a shopping bag, so she did."

"That can't be right," I told him. "You can hardly get *people* past airport security checks now."

"She came off a boat," said Crusher. "It's different with boats. And she fed it some of

her sleeping pills so that it didn't move. They must have thought it was a soft toy or something."

I looked again at the alligator. It *was* a bit like a big soft toy, lying in the straw. Its eyes were kind of half open, as if it was dreaming.

I didn't know then that it was it still crammed full of sleeping pills.

I didn't know that it was going to be a whole different beast when those tablets wore off and it woke up, mad with hunger.

Chapter 3

Only a Fiver

"You can pat it if you like," said Crusher. "Go on. Don't be scared. It won't harm you."

He lifted the box out of his car boot. He placed it on the ground beside me. I knelt down, put my hand in and stroked the

alligator. Its skin wasn't as rough as it looked.

"What's it called?" I asked him.

"Don't be a goofball, Jono. It's an alligator, so it's called an alligator."

"I know it's an alligator," I said. "I mean, has it got a name?"

Crusher rolled his eyes. "You buy it, Jono. You can call it what you like."

"I'm not buying an alligator," I said. "What would I do with an alligator?"

"It would be a very different sort of pet," said Crusher. "No one else would have anything like it."

"And I'm not going to have anything like it either," I replied, "just think what my mum would say if I came home with an alligator."

"I'll only charge you a fiver."

15

"A fiver!" I laughed. "You must be joking. For me to take that alligator off your hands *you* would need to give *me* the fiver."

"Done!" said Crusher at once.

He reached in his pocket, took out a fiver, and shoved it into my hand. Then he kicked the box over to me, jumped in his car and drove away.

Chapter 4

Gullible

Crusher had fooled me. Gullible, that's what I am.

Do you know that the word *gullible* is not in the dictionary?

This is a trick question.

See, now you have to say. "*Gullible*! Not in the dictionary! I'm amazed. Are you sure?"

Then *I* say, "No, really, that's the truth. The word *gullible* is not in the dictionary."

At this point I hand you a dictionary. "Check it out for yourself," I tell you.

So then, you look up the word *gullible* in the dictionary.

And it says –

Gullible: easily taken in or tricked.

Get it?

Duh!

My mates in my class did this to me. Several times.

My mum says that by the third or fourth time even I should have twigged what they were up to.

But they kept bringing different dictionaries. And the last time they said,

19

"Honest, Jono, this is a *children's* dictionary. It's not there. See for yourself."

And I thought maybe it wasn't this time, because it was a children's dictionary, and I looked it up.

You see how gullible I am.

Chapter 5

Internet Check

I'm not good with words. I don't really like them.

And not just the word *gullible*. I don't like any of them.

Words are confusing. I get them mixed up when I try to read things. And I never know how to spell them right.

The teachers all say, "Use your dictionary."

But you need to know how to spell to use a dictionary. Computers are better. I use mine all the time.

So when I got home I decided to find out some facts about my alligator on the Internet. He was still sleeping in his box so I

put him in our garden shed. Then I went
inside and logged on to our computer. The
good thing about the Internet is that you can
look something up even if you're not sure
how to spell it.

I type in A.L.L.Y. G.A.T.E. O.R.

And after a second the screen flashes,

Do you mean ALLIGATOR?

A few clicks and I've got it.

There's a picture of an alligator. With some text beside it. I can read enough words to get the meaning.

And I'm not happy.

I'm not happy at all.

Chapter 6

Facts About Alligators

My mum came home as I was printing out the fact sheets on alligators.

"My feet are killing me," she said, pulling off her shoes. "I'm too tired to cook tonight. Fancy something from the chippie?"

"Fine," I said, even though I knew it meant that I would have to walk round to the chip shop.

"What's this, Jono?" She picked up the computer print-out.

"School project," I said at once.

It's the best answer if an adult asks why you're on the Internet. You just say "school project" and they say, "Oh, right. OK."

"Oh, right. OK," said my mum.

I put the computer print-out in my school folder.

"It's good that the project is about something you're interested in," said my mum. "You always liked animals, from when you were a little boy."

"So why did you never let me have a pet?" I asked her.

"Your dad had allergies, and then, and then," she stumbled a bit, "when he died, well, I'm out at work every day and you're at school. I suppose you're older now, and if you promised you'd take proper care of it ..."

"I would. I would," I said.

"I'll think about it." She laughed. "As long as you don't ask me for a pet alligator."

I had a quick peek in the shed on my way to the chippie. As I lifted the lid of the box the alligator moved its head. It was beginning to wake up.

It raised one eyelid and stared at me with its big yellow eye.

Chapter 7

A Hungry Alligator

I was only gone for about 15 minutes.

I didn't know a hungry alligator could do that much damage in 15 minutes.

On my way back from the chippie I thought I'd go into our garden shed to have another look. As I opened the shed door the barbecue stand crashed down and ash blew all over the place. The alligator was loose!

It grabbed a whole chunk of garden hose pipe and bit clean through it. Then it turned its head and saw me. It lashed out with its tail, and opened its big jaws. There were enormous rows of teeth along each side. I screamed and dropped the take-away.

I just got out of there in time. I slammed the door and put a big stone up against it. I watched through the hut window as the

alligator ate the chicken supper, the two single fish, the pizza with double chips and curry sauce, the portion of onion rings, and all the boxes they came in.

That seemed to calm it down. It snuffled around a bit and then lay still. But if my print-out from the Internet was right it wasn't even half grown yet. It would rest now, but when it woke up it would be starving again.

Chapter 8

An Idea

I still had the fiver Crusher gave me so I ran back to the shop and bought another two meals for me and my mum.

"Sam's coming round later," she said as we ate our dinner.

Since my dad died my mum's had a few boy-friends. None of them lasted very long. Then Sam turned up. He does car repairs. He has his own work-shop in a lock-up garage near the old railway line. He's OK.

We were clearing up when Sam came in. He'd got a new DVD.

"I thought we could watch this together," he said.

"I've got to go out for a while," I muttered. "Just go ahead without me."

"Sam's trying to make friends with you, Jono," my mum whispered to me.

"I know," I said. "I'll come back later and watch the end of it with you." I couldn't explain to her that I had an alligator to take care of.

"Suit yourself, Jono," said Sam. He dropped his keys on the kitchen table and took off his jacket.

"I won't be long," I said.

I had a sudden idea what I might do with the alligator.

Chapter 9

A Good Hiding Place

Sam and my mum went into the living room to watch the DVD.

I crept into the kitchen and took Sam's keys from the table. Then I went out to the garden shed. I checked that the alligator was sleeping before I opened the door.

I heaved the alligator into my dad's old golf bag and slung the bag onto my back. I hurried out of our garden and across the road towards Sam's lock-up. It was getting dark, so no one saw the alligator tail peeking out the top of the bag.

When I got to the lock-up garages I knew which one was Sam's. It had his name and mobile number painted on the shutter. I opened the door and went inside. I stood over the car pit and tipped the alligator into it.

That would keep the alligator safe until I could decide what to do with him.

I locked up carefully and went home. I put Sam's keys on the hall table and sat down on the couch beside him and my mum to watch the DVD.

Chapter 10

Thief!

We had just got to a really exciting part of the film, when Sam's mobile went off.

Sam jumped up from the couch. "It's the police. There's a bit of trouble at my lock-up!" he cried out. "I'll need to go round there right now!"

I picked up his keys from the hall table and gave them to him. Sam took them and ran out of the house. Mum and I ran after him.

Two police-men were at the lock-up. They had arrested a man who had broken in to steal a car Sam was working on.

The thief was yelling. "There's a monster in there! A giant alligator!"

"That's rubbish," said Sam. "As if anyone in their right mind would keep an alligator in a lock-up!"

47

"We've heard lots of stories in our time," said one police-man, "but this one beats them all."

"I'm telling you, it's true," the thief shouted. "Take a look for yourselves if you don't believe me."

Sam and Mum and me went inside the lock-up.

The other police-man put the thief in the police car.

The first police-man came with us. He
pulled out his notebook. "I'll just get ready to
take down this alligator's details," he joked.

Sam switched on the light. There was a
scrabbling sound coming from the car pit.
We all went over and looked down.

My mum screamed. "It *is* an alligator!"

Sam's mouth fell open. "How did that get
in there?" he said.

The police-man stared at the alligator. He put his notebook back in his pocket. He scratched his head and winked at Sam. "I'm sure an alligator is a lot better than a guard dog," he said. "But I think you should call the zoo and get them to take it away."

Chapter 11

Smart Boy

Sam called the zoo and they said they would be with us in an hour.

A man and a woman arrived. We watched as they caught the alligator with a big net and put him in a van. The woman said there was a good chance the zoo would keep him and we could come and visit him.

After we got home my mum gave me a hard look. She said, "I find it a bit funny that you were checking facts about alligators on the Internet tonight and then suddenly there's an alligator in Sam's lock-up. Is there anything you want to tell me, Jono?"

"Oh, leave Jono alone," said Sam. "Where would he get an alligator from?"

When Mum went to make a cup of tea Sam spoke to me in a low voice.

"I know it was you, Jono," he said. "I left my keys on the kitchen table. But when we were going out to the lock-up, you picked them up from the hall table."

So I told Sam about Crusher and how I had to find somewhere safe to put the alligator.

"I'm glad you hid in it my lock-up," said Sam. "If that car had been stolen I'd have lost a lot of money."

Sam slipped 20 quid into my pocket.

"You're a smart boy, Jono," he said.

Chapter 12

A Surprise

Sam says he's going to get a dog to guard the lock-up. Mum says it can stay at our house some of the time and I can look after it and take it for walks.

I haven't told them yet what happened when I went back to clear up the mess in the shed. It was weeks and weeks before I got round to doing this.

There was a whole lot of goo and other stuff scrunched up inside the cardboard box. I was dragging the box outside to dump it in the bin, when I saw something lying under the straw.

I picked it up.

It was round and smooth to touch. I felt something move inside.

Then I knew what it was.

It was an egg.

An alligator egg.

Barrington Stoke would like to thank all its readers for commenting on the manuscript before publication and in particular:

Lizzie Alder
Karla Louise Allen
Beatriz Amaral
Scott Braaten
Milo Bright
Oscar Browne
Emmelina Cecchini
Hannah Cone
Ashley Davis
Fiona Duncan
Jon Freeman
Stefan Gauci
Theresa Gauci
Ryan Growden
Jack Hart
Aleksander Hass
Kylie Hawke
Ashley van der Heyden
Alistair Hornsby
Nathan Hughes
Kanako Igarishi
Sophia Johnsen
Abigail Kent
Aleksi Lehtinen
Emilia Ludwig
Kanna Marukawa
Franziska Meier
Amy Peat
Adam Preece
Ariagni Prokakis
Gareth Redington
Daniel Reichling
Elizabeth Reilly
Lotte Schol
Nancy Squiccianarini
Lindsay Stone
Zofia Tokaj
Will Triebel
Mary Ruth Wagner
Matt Wagner
Ryan Watkins
Niall Wiley
Emmie Williams

Become a Consultant!

Would you like to give us feedback on our titles before they are published? Contact us at the email address below – we'd love to hear from you!

info@barringtonstoke.co.uk
www.barringtonstoke.co.uk